Baby

new seasons™

Original inspirations by Judy Hershner, Marie Jones, and Ellen F. Pill.

Compiled inspirations by Karen Barker Crowley.

Publications International, Ltd., has made every effort to locate the owners of all copyrighted material to obtain permission to use the selections that appear in this book. Any errors or omissions are unintentional; corrections, if necessary, will be made in future editions.

Excerpt from *The Day We Met You* by Phoebe Koehler. Copyright © 1990 by Phoebe Koehler. Reprinted by permission of Simon & Schuster Books for Young Readers, an imprint of Simon & Schuster Children's Publishing Division.

Excerpt from *Waiting for Baby* by Tom Birdseye. Copyright © 1991 by Tom Birdseye. Reprinted by permission of Holiday House, Inc.

Excerpt from *A Mother's Story* by Gloria Vanderbilt. Copyright © 1996 by Gloria Vanderbilt. Reprinted by permission of Alfred A. Knopf, a subsidiary of Random House, Inc.

Excerpt from *The Sense of Wonder* by Rachel L. Carson. Copyright © 1956 by Rachel L. Carson. Copyright © renewed 1984 by Roger Christie. Reprinted by permission of Frances Collin, Trustee.

Front cover and additional photography by Sacco Productions Limited/Chicago; SuperStock.

Illustrations by Jane A. Dippold, Judy Nowka, Jan Palmer, Judith Pfeiffer, and Joyce Shelton.

Louis Weber, CEO
Publications International, Ltd.
7373 North Cicero Avenue
Lincolnwood, Illinois 60712

Permission is never granted for commercial purposes.

Manufactured in China.

8 7 6 5 4 3 2 1

ISBN: 0-7853-5221-X

he minute we saw you we knew that we loved you.
You felt like the sun shining inside us.

PHOEBE KOEHLER, *THE DAY WE MET YOU*

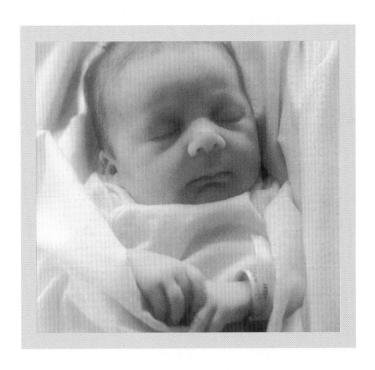

Babies teach us to live in the present, where all of life's magic exists.

How is it possible that someone with such tiny hands can have such a firm grip on my heart?

The soft tininess
of a baby reminds
us how very small a
miracle can be.

Our Photo

... I'm holding you. And I'm loving you.
Because you're finally, *finally* together with me.

TOM BIRDSEYE, *WAITING FOR BABY*

Sleep, my baby, sleep—
as the stars watch over
your gentle tranquility,
bringing you sweet,
heavenly dreams.

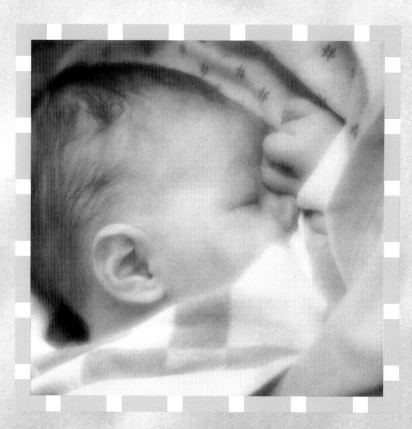

$\mathcal{A}$ lullaby is
simply a parent's
love set to music.

I want to give everything to you,
my sweet child:

spring's dewy raindrops,

summer's soft warmth,

autumn's gentle briskness,

winter's cool beauty . . .

all the seasons of a richly woven life.

eyes

babies

Babies have big eyes to

help them behold a world

world

that is entirely new.

new

All children are born
innocent and good. In this
sense our children
are from heaven.

JOHN GRAY, PH.D.,
CHILDREN ARE FROM HEAVEN

Babies seem to have dimples everywhere.
Those must be the places where angels kissed them.

When you gently tickle a
baby, listen carefully!
You will hear angels giggling
and cherubs cooing with joy.

When I held my newborn
son for the first time, I looked
in awe and wonder at every
inch of him. How could it be
that his hands were empty,
when I could tell for certain
that he held my heart firmly
in his grasp?

*C*an anything in heaven
or earth be softer than
my baby's skin,
sweeter than her scent?

When a baby cries, a mother

feels the protective pull of

thousands of years of instinct.

When a baby smiles, a

mother feels a love that

knows no beginning or end.

Our Photo

You are my baby. You can see it in our smiles.

Babies are made of
tickles and charm,
stardust and sunbeams,
snuggles and promise.

Ten tiny fingers and ten tiny toes,
soft petal lips and a cute button nose,
a sweet sassy laugh and a smile so coy,
all lovingly wrapped in a bundle of joy.

I hold you in my arms, convinced that I have never truly known the meaning of love until now.

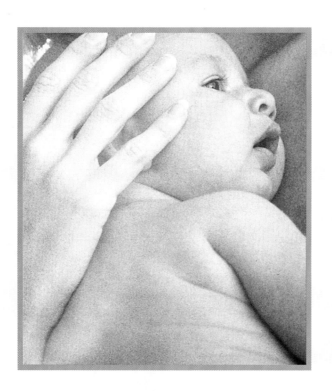

$\mathcal{A}$ baby combines the
hopes of past generations with the
dreams of future possibilities.

Caring for a baby
is like opening a
treasure chest

full of shiny, new
experiences

and precious,
priceless moments.

Baby doesn't care how much money you have or what you do for a living. Baby knows that the secret to happiness comes from love and life's simple pleasures.

During your first year you will experience so many
new things, such as your first foods, first words, and first
steps, but you won't be able to remember those events.
Don't worry, though—we will remember for you.

Baby's first steps make your heart run,
skip, and jump.

$\mathcal{M}$ay sweet lullabies echo
in your heart forever.

$\mathcal{D}$ear Guardian Angel—
Watch over this
precious child
with special care,
for this is my baby,
this is my love.

$\mathcal{W}$hat do babies dream about? Probably their dreams
are filled with impressions of soft blankets, warm milk,
and Mother's gentle touch. No wonder babies smile
when they're sleeping!

To be pregnant has been for me each time the supreme joy. It is my greatest achievement, . . . I never felt so centered, so beautiful, so loved, so important. I loved my body and my spirit as never before. Each day came as a miracle.

GLORIA VANDERBILT, *A MOTHER'S STORY*

A new baby in your life changes
everything: You'll have much more work and
much less sleep, and you'll discover within
yourself an ability to love that is beyond
anything you could have imagined!

A baby combines

the hopes of past

generations with the

dreams of future

possibilities.

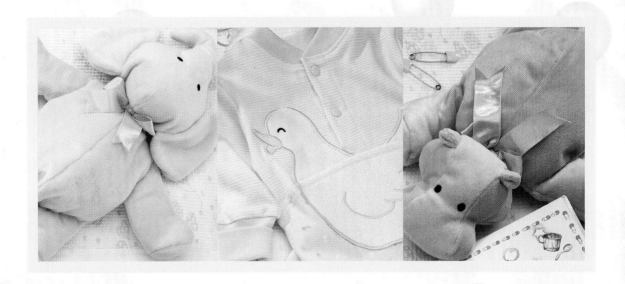

$\mathcal{B}$abies are necessary to grown-ups.
A new baby is like the beginning of all things—
wonder, hope, a dream of possibilities.

EDA J. LESHAN

It is impossible to hold a baby in your arms
without feeling a light envelop both of you.

I never knew how much love
    my heart could contain.
I never knew how strong a bond could be.
I never knew—until I knew you.

Baby's Photo

Beautiful

Awe-inspiring

Baby

You

$\mathcal{W}$hen the first baby
laughed for the first time,
the laugh broke into a thousand
pieces and they all went
skipping about, and that was
the beginning of fairies.

SIR JAMES MATTHEWS BARRIE, *PETER PAN*

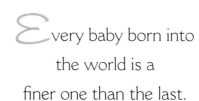

Every baby born into
the world is a
finer one than the last.

CHARLES DICKENS,
NICHOLAS NICKLEBY

A baby's soul comes
straight from the twinkle in
God's loving eye.

One of our favorite activities is memorizing each other's faces.

Every family member finds their own reflection in the face of the new baby.

Sparkling like the first star of evening,
a baby's eyes glitter with all that is bright.

We have so many things to teach you, little one: how to walk and speak, how to take care of yourself, and how to make good choices in life. But the most important lesson we will ever teach you is this: You are loved.

One of the great things about babies is that they teach their parents just as much about life as their parents teach them.

*W*ithin the glow
of each new baby
lies the promise of
a world that knows peace.

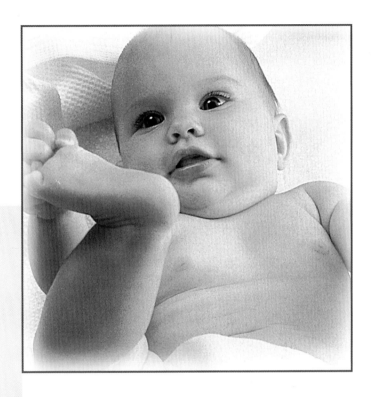

Tiny, tender baby,

so quiet and so wise,

I see the promise of tomorrow

when I look into your eyes.

There is no greater joy than looking into
your baby's eyes and seeing your own reflection,
your own hopes and dreams.

own reflection

baby's eyes

hopes and dreams

promise

$\mathcal{R}$emember you are the promise

and the hope of the future. future

Remember you are the very

essence of life. born

Remember you are born for

a purpose.

purpose

Since it will be a while
before you understand
the words *I love you,*
I'll just have to show you
how I feel with a
thousand hugs and kisses.

To touch a baby is to understand just how
wonderful and precious life is.

A baby's smile brings
a moment of
perfection and balance;
it is a reminder of all that
is absolute in this
beautiful world.

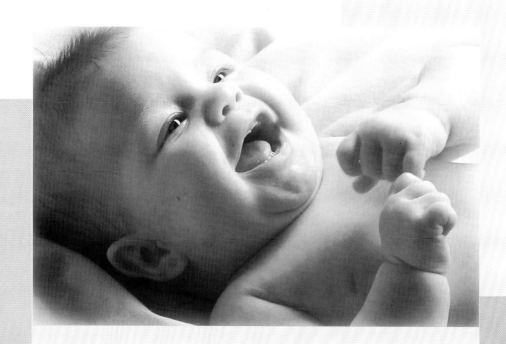

The sweetest flowers
in all the world—
A baby's hands.

ALGERNON CHARLES
SWINBURNE

Baby's Photo

I love to watch you kick your
froggy legs and smile one of your
toothless grins.

$\mathcal{W}$hen you wave your tiny arms
back and forth with so much enthusiasm,
it looks as though you are
conducting an invisible orchestra.

$\mathcal{B}$abies are angels in training,
blessings in diapers and bibs.

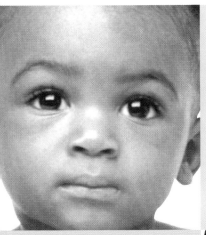

$\mathcal{B}$abies are God's most precious creative handiwork, each one a unique expression of pure love and unlimited potential.

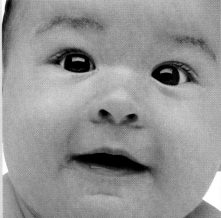

$\mathcal{I}$f I had influence with the good fairy
who is supposed to preside over the
christening of all children, I should ask
that her gift to each child in the world
be a sense of wonder so indestructible
that it would last throughout life....

RACHEL CARSON, *THE SENSE OF WONDER*

Parents' love for their baby knows no boundaries.
Parents' hope for their baby sees no limitations.

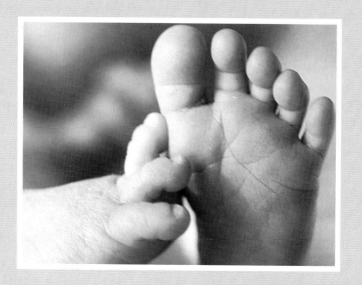

$\mathcal{N}$ewborns are just as miraculous today as they were decades or even centuries ago. Those ten tiny fingers and ten tiny toes are just as astonishing as they ever were.

STAN AND JAN BERENSTAIN, *WHAT YOUR PARENTS NEVER TOLD YOU ABOUT BEING A MOM OR DAD*

To carry a baby within you is to know love.

To give birth to a baby is to know awe.

To watch your child grow and prosper is to know true joy.

With love and wonder

To

From

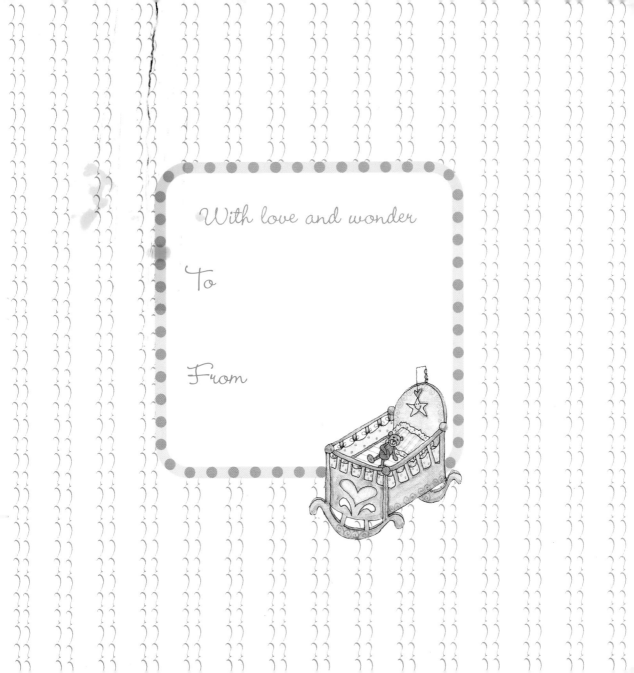